Taylor's Pocket Guide to

Modern Roses

Taylor's Pocket Guide to

Modern
Roses

ANN REILLY
Consulting Editor

A Chanticleer Press Edition
Houghton Mifflin Company
Boston

For information about
permission to reproduce selections from this book,
write to Permissions,
Houghton Mifflin Company, 2 Park Street,
Boston, Massachusetts 02108.

Based on Taylor's Encyclopedia of Gardening, Fourth Edition,
Copyright © 1961 by Norman Taylor,
revised and edited by
Gordon P. DeWolf, Jr.

Prepared and produced by Chanticleer Press, New York
Typeset by Dix Type, Inc., Syracuse, New York
Printed and bound by
Dai Nippon, Tokyo, Japan

Library of Congress Catalog Card Number: 88-46144
ISBN: 0-395-51017-1

00   10   9   8   7   6   5   4   3   2   1

CONTENTS

GARDENING WITH
MODERN ROSES

THROUGHOUT history, roses have been the most cherished of flowers, universally loved for their delicacy, beauty, color, fragrance, and elegance. Growing roses will bring you the greatest of pleasures. Most blend well into a variety of settings. They can serve as an architectural feature—covering trellises or buildings—or be strictly ornamental. You can add roses to a special fragrance garden, planting them among herbs, or use them in hedges to create privacy and elegance in one stroke. There is a rose for every situation, from the most formal garden to the most informal backyard.

Roses do not need to stand on their own. They may be combined with annuals, perennials, or shrubs, so that even the smallest garden can have roses. Spring-flowering bulbs planted between rose bushes will bring early color to the beds. Where space is very limited, a miniature rose garden still allows you to enjoy the "queen of the flowers."

Rose Classification

Roses are placed in different classes, based on their ancestry. From the point of view of the beginning gardener, the class to which a modern rose belongs makes little actual difference, with the exception of the miniatures. But members of each class tend to have certain characteristics—flower form, hardiness, height, and the like—that may influence your decision in choosing rose bushes.

All of the roses in this book are varieties that have been developed since about the middle of the 19th century. On the basis of its ancestry, each is placed in one of four major classes: hybrid teas, floribundas, grandiflora, and miniatures.

The hybrid teas are the oldest of the four groups in modern cultivation; their development, considered to have begun with the introduction of La France in 1867, is generally acknowledged as the beginning of the era of modern roses. Hybrid teas are also the most popular class of rose, with classic, high-centered blossoms borne on long stems.

The first floribunda was introduced in the 1920s. These roses resulted from a cross of hybrid teas with older, smaller-flowered roses called polyanthas, producing hardy plants with a multitude of flowers per stem.

The grandifloras are a small group; the class was created in the middle of this century for the hybrid Queen Elizabeth, a rose that combined the best of the hybrid teas and the floribundas. The tall-growing grandifloras bear teeming clusters of large flowers with the classic hybrid-tea form.

Miniature roses, although known in the early 19th century, became lost in rose culture for a time; they reemerged as a class in the 1920s. Since that time, miniatures have rapidly increased in popularity; their flowers are often perfect small reproductions of those of their splendid larger cousins, and many are well suited to growing as patio or container plants.

In this book, the four classes are arranged alphabetically; within each class, individual plant descriptions are organized by color and shape of the flowers.

Getting Started

The roses included in this book are all widely available and grown extensively in the United States. After making a preliminary selection from these pages, you may want to attend the rose shows of societies in your neighborhood or obtain and study catalogues from leading mail-order nurseries. Rose enthusiasts in your region will be glad to offer you advice and encouragement.

Selecting Varieties

The number of rose bushes you plant will depend largely on two factors—the available space and the amount of time you wish to devote to them. For beginning gardeners, it is wise to start small; by planting just four to six rose bushes you will learn the basics of rose maintenance, and you will also give yourself the chance to try out two or three different varieties.

The first important consideration in growing beautiful roses, and something often overlooked by the beginner, is to start out with good plants. Purchase your roses either from a reputable mail-order company or from a reliable nursery or garden shop.

Don't assume that high-priced roses are necessarily the best. The price of patented, newer hybrids includes a royalty; older varieties or cultivars, which have stood the test of time, may do just as well and are often less expensive.

The American Rose Society publishes a booklet called the "Handbook for Selecting Roses," which rates all roses on a scale from 1 to 10, based on members' comments. This too is a good guide in selecting varieties; any variety rated over 7.5 would be a good choice. Members also receive a monthly magazine and an annual yearbook. The Society has many other programs of benefit to rose growers; contact them at P.O. Box 30,000, Shreveport, LA 71130 for further information.

What to Look For

Roses are graded (1, 1½, or 2) in accordance with established standards laid down in 1923 and revised periodically since then. The highest grade is Grade 1, but whichever you purchase, be sure that the plant you buy has a robust, well-developed root system. The canes should not be shriveled or blackened or show any other sign of damage; the bark should be green and the pith white or nearly white. Look for healthy growth or growth buds. If you purchase Grade 1½ roses, you should pay less for these than you would for Grade 1 plants.

Planning Your Rose Garden

Roses need plenty of room and should be planted well away from existing trees and shrubs with which they will compete for sunlight, water, and nutrients. If a tree or shrub in your yard is not yet fully grown, attempt to visualize its size in five or ten years before you plant your roses.

Roses need at least six to eight hours of full sunlight each day. If there is a choice of morning or afternoon sun, choose morning sun, which will decrease the possibility of disease problems. Afternoon shade protects the plants from too much summer heat and retards the drying out of the soil.

A rose bed can be almost any size or shape you like—rectangular, square, circular, or curving. The choice depends on the available space and your preference for a formal or informal look. Do not make it so large that you cannot reach into the center of the bed to care for the inner plants.

Preparing the Soil

Next in importance to a good plant is good soil. If you are not sure about the quality of your soil, take a soil sample and have it analyzed by a private laboratory or your county agent. These experts can instruct you as to how to prepare the sample and will give you recommendations for correcting deficiencies, if there are any.

Soil pH, a measure of the soil acidity or alkalinity, should be between 6.5 and 6.8, although roses will tolerate a pH of 6.0 to 7.5. If you have your soil professionally analyzed, the pH level will be reported. If not, your garden center may be able to do it for you, or you can purchase a soil pH test kit.

If your soil pH is not at the correct level, add agricultural lime or dolomitic limestone to raise the pH, or sulfur to lower it. Your garden center or the package label will give you instructions as to how much to apply. Distribute the material evenly over the bed and mix it into the soil well.

If you are preparing new beds, you must first remove the grass and any stones or debris that may be in the soil. Next add organic matter, such as peat moss, leaf mold, compost, or well-rotted cow manure, in an amount so that it will be 25 percent of the final soil mixture. In very sandy soil, add up to 50 percent organic matter. Most soils in North America need additional phosphorus. Bone meal or superphosphate, both sources of the phosphorus needed for good root growth, should be added according to label instructions. Mix all components into the soil with a spade or tiller to a depth of 18–24 inches.

Roses like well-drained and well-aerated soil. Heavy clay soils benefit from the addition of gypsum, which keeps the soil from retaining too much moisture. Sharp sand or vermiculite may also be used to improve drainage and aeration. In areas with very heavy soils, it is often a good idea to raise the beds three to six inches off the ground, or install drainage tiles.

If possible, prepare your beds in the fall prior to planting the following spring. You can prepare beds in spring, but you must wait until after the soil is no longer cold and wet.

Planting Bare-Root Roses

Bare-root roses, obtained from mail-order houses and some garden centers, are dormant plants packed with a protective material around the roots to keep them from drying out. Once you receive your roses, you must keep them in a cool, dark place until you are ready to plant them. You can hold them for up to two weeks in the box if the roots are kept damp in a plastic bag. If you must hold them longer than this, you will have to bury them in a trench, a process called "heeling in."

Before planting, rose roots should be soaked in a bucket of water for 24 hours to restore any lost moisture. When you are ready to plant, remove the plants one at a time. Examine the roots and remove any that are broken or damaged with pruning shears.

Inspect the canes and remove any that are broken or weak. If the tops of any canes have dried out, these tops should also be removed. Cut the canes down to one-quarter inch above the next outward-facing bud, cutting at a 45-degree angle away from the bud.

For each bush, dig a hole 18 inches deep and 18 inches across. If the plant is too large for the hole, either make the hole a little larger or prune the roots back slightly. Replace enough of the soil in the hole to form a pyramid or mound whose top is even with the soil level. Place the plant on the mound, spreading the roots as evenly as possible and situating it so that the bud union (the knot of wood between the canes and the roots) is at or just below the soil level.

Fill in the hole until it is about three-quarters full, and tamp down the soil gently around the roots with your hands. Fill the hole with water and allow it to drain. When the hole is empty of water, fill it in with the remaining soil and add water again.

Build a mound of soil over the canes to about three-quarters of their length to keep them from drying out until growth starts. There should be enough soil mixture left to do this; if not, use moistened peat moss or other organic matter and keep it moist until growth starts. Once the buds have started to grow and are about two inches long, gently remove the soil mound with a stream of water.

Planting Potted Roses

Many roses sold by garden centers come in pots made of plastic, compressed peat, or biodegradable paper. Sometimes these bushes will be in active growth and possibly in bud or bloom. It is important when planting these roses to disturb the root system as little as possible.

Before planting, water the pot thoroughly. Prepare the soil and dig the hole in the same manner as for bare-root roses. Place the rose and its pot in the hole and fill in around it with soil mixture. Then lift the plant, pot and all, from the hole. Carefully take the plant out of the pot and place it into the space left in the hole.

If the soil starts to fall away from the roots when you start to remove the pot, return the plant to the pot, cut out the bottom surface, and make several slits into the sides of the pot. Holding the plant by the bottom, ease it into the hole, remove the sides of the pot, and tamp the soil gently around the roots. Water well. If the plant is actively growing, soil does not need to be mounded up over the canes as described for bare-root roses. If the plant is still dormant, it will benefit from the soil mound until growth starts.

To lessen transplanting shock, remove any flowers or buds so that the plant's energy goes into establishing the roots.

Planting Miniature Roses

Miniature roses are usually sold in containers and are planted the same way as other potted roses. The holes will naturally not need to be as large.

Planting Distances

The distance between your roses depends on the type of rose and the climate. In the North, hybrid teas, grandifloras, and spreading floribundas are planted 24 inches apart. Smaller floribundas and floribundas used as hedges are planted 18 inches apart. Miniatures are spaced according to their ultimate size, with smaller ones as close as 6–8 inches apart and the larger ones 12 inches apart.

In the South, where plants will grow larger, space hybrid teas, grandifloras, and spreading floribundas 36 inches apart. Smaller floribundas and those for hedging are spaced 24–30 inches apart, and miniatures anywhere from 8 to 18 inches apart, based on their ultimate size.

In the North, situate large plants 9–12 inches back from the edge of the bed; increase this distance by half a foot in the South. Miniatures should be set back four to eight inches, depending on their size. Setting your plants back is especially important where there will be foot traffic along the side of the beds, to protect passersby from the thorns.

Give your roses plenty of room. Overcrowded roses will not develop properly and may be more susceptible to the spread of disease. In beds with three or more rows of plants, staggering the bushes will make for a more attractive arrangement and give each bush a larger space in which to develop more evenly.

Transplanting Roses

Roses may be transplanted in much the same way that bare-root roses are planted. Transplanting must be done when the plants are dormant, either in early spring, or, where winter temperatures do not drop below 0° F, in the late fall. When digging plants for transplanting, be careful to keep the roots as intact as possible.

Pruning and Other Important Techniques

To have strong, healthy rose bushes, it is essential to learn how to prune them. The most severe pruning is done in spring, but continues throughout the growing season as spent blooms are removed.

Buy a good pair of scissor-type pruning shears, or secateurs, and keep them sharp. Do not use anvil shears, which can crush the canes. Hold the hook edge of the secateurs above the cutting blade so that if any crushing occurs, it will only damage the piece of the cane being cut off.

Prune in early spring when the growth buds start to swell but before they have fully leafed out. First remove any dead canes or those that are damaged by disease, cutting them flush with the bud union. Next remove any canes that are weak or smaller than a pencil in diameter, or those that are growing into the center of the plant. After that, examine your bush.

Select three or four of the newest and healthiest-looking canes and remove all the others, cutting them flush with the bud union. On floribundas and miniatures planted for mass color effect, five or six canes can be left on the plant.

The next step is to cut canes down to their proper height. For large roses, a good rule of thumb is to cut them to 12–14 inches in the North and 18–24 inches in the South. Winter kill may necessitate cutting canes shorter than this. If the tops of the canes have been winter killed, cut them down to where they are green on the outside or with white or nearly white pith on the inside. Prune miniatures to a height of three to six inches, depending on their ultimate height.

When pruning the canes, cut them one-quarter inch above an outward-facing bud, at a 45-degree angle. Doing so will keep the plant in better shape and avoids having canes crisscrossing in the center of the plant.

Some areas of the country have a problem with insects that bore into rose canes and eventually kill them. If you note this occurrence, you should seal all canes with tree-wound paint or shellac after you cut them.

Several weeks after you have finished pruning, take another hard look at your plants. Canes may die back somewhat after pruning from unexpected cold or canker disease; if you note damaged canes, simply prune again to remove the damage.

When pruning is completed, the canes should form a bowl radiating from the center of the bush. The center will be open to sunlight, and the shape encourages basal breaks from the bud union. During the growing season, check the plant to ensure that no canes are growing toward the center; if any develop, cut them out.

Suckers

Keep an eye out for suckers, which are canes that grow from the understock beneath the bud union. They are easy to recognize because their foliage is distinct from that of the top part of the plant. They must be removed, because they will eventually take over the plant. Trace their source to under the bud union and cut them off there.

Preventing Disease

After pruning, clean up all debris and old leaves from the ground. Many organisms that transmit diseases overwinter in this debris; its removal will not eliminate problems but will reduce them during the summer.

Thumb Pruning

Occasionally, two or more bud eyes will grow from the same point. This results in crowding and weaker canes, and requires that the extra bud eyes be removed so that only one remains. Unwanted eyes may also grow in the wrong place or in the wrong direction. When they are small, you can thumb-prune, or remove them with your fingers.

Disbudding

If you want your hybrid teas or grandifloras to produce long cutting stems with one flower per stem, you may need to disbud your roses. Examine your plants as soon as flower buds appear. If more than one bud surrounds the central bud, it is simple to remove them with your fingers when they are still small. If they are left to grow naturally, a cluster of flowers will appear.

On floribundas, the central flower always blooms and fades before the surrounding ones bloom, leaving a hole in the center of the cluster when the rest of the flowers come into bloom. You can prevent this uneven-looking cluster from developing by removing the central bud on floribundas as soon as it appears.

Cutting Fresh Roses

You should not take garden roses indoors until after the green, leaflike sepals have fallen away from the bud. Roses will have a longer vase life if you cut them when they are no more than one-third open. When cutting flowers, make your incision one-quarter inch above a five-leaflet leaf, at a 45-degree angle away from the leaf; be sure to keep at least two leaves on any cane when cutting new blooms from it. Put the stem into water immediately.

Dead-heading

Removing faded flowers is known as dead-heading. It is important to remove flowers as soon as they have passed their peak to keep them from going to seed and to encourage new growth quickly. Using pruning shears, cut the stem back to the first five-leaflet leaf, one-quarter inch above the leaf at a 45-degree angle away from the leaf. When canes are very long, they may be cut down lower than the first leaf, provided at least two five-leaflet leaves are left on the cane.

When cutting fresh flowers or dead-heading, you must treat first-year plants somewhat differently. To strengthen the plant, cuts should not be made lower than the first five-leaflet leaf. Some gardeners cut buds off new plants before they open, so that the plant does not even bloom during its first cycle. This practice directs all of the plant's strength into root and cane production and results in a stronger plant.

Treating New Canes

New canes that develop from the bud union are called basal breaks. These may develop in spring when growth starts or during the growing season, especially after the first bloom cycle. Sometimes the new basals grow quite tall; being succulent in growth, they can break off easily. It would be wise either to prune these canes back when they reach the height of the rest of the plant, or to stake them.

New canes, especially on hybrid teas, form large flower clusters known as candelabras. These have small flowers and short stems. If the cane is pruned to the first five-leaflet leaf as the candelabra buds appear, new side shoots will appear and the end result will be a better-shaped and more abundantly flowering plant.

Watering

Roses can withstand periods of dry weather, but they will grow more quickly and produce larger and more colorful flowers if they receive adequate water. Water your roses deeply at least once a week, and more frequently if it is hot. If the rainfall in your area is inadequate, at least one inch of water should be applied weekly. Roses should have plenty of water from the time growth starts in spring until the first fall frost.

There are several methods of watering roses. In the morning, plants may be watered with an overhead sprinkler, but later in the day overhead water will keep the foliage wet through the night, encouraging disease. Serious rose growers use soaker hoses or underground irrigation to eliminate wet foliage and flowers.

Mulching

It is a good idea to mulch your roses. Mulches keep the ground cooler in the hot summer, help to retain soil moisture, and eliminate some weeds. Organic mulching materials are recommended because they will enrich the soil as they break down; shredded leaves, bark chips, buckwheat or cocoa hulls, and leaf mold are all good materials. (Never use straight peat moss as a mulch; it can dry out quickly and be difficult to rewet, causing severe problems.)

Apply two to four inches of mulch in mid-spring, as soon as the ground is warm.

Controlling Weeds

Weeds compete fiercely with roses for water and nutrients, and they can harbor insects and diseases, so they should be removed as soon as they appear. Using an organic mulch will help you avoid having continually to remove weeds by hand. As an alternative, spread black plastic over the ground, punching holes into it so water can penetrate. Cover the plastic with an organic mulch to hide it.

There are products called preemergent herbicides, available at garden centers, that kill weed seeds before they germinate. These products will not harm your roses; they can be applied in mid-spring and again as necessary during the summer. Be very careful with post-emergent herbicides; some can cause extreme damage to the roses. Consult with the experts at your garden center for the best products to use.

Fertilizing Your Roses

Roses are heavy feeders—that is, they like to be fed often. Choose a fertilizer designed for roses or for other flowering plants. There are three numbers on a fertilizer label; they tell you the percentage of nitrogen, phosphorus, and potash present in the mixture. For roses, the appropriate mixture is a fertilizer whose second number is the same as or higher than the first, such as 10–10–10 or 5–10–5.

Apply the first fertilizer as soon as the roses are pruned in the spring. For best growth, make at least two other applications, once after the first cycle of bloom has finished and again two months later. For maximum effect, fertilize once a month from early spring until two months before the first fall frost.

When applying fertilizer, follow label directions for the amount to apply, and spread the fertilizer evenly over the soil. Scratch it lightly into the soil and water it in well. Do not allow fertilizer to touch the bud union. If the ground is dry, water it before putting the fertilizer down. Fertilizer can be spread on top of mulch provided it is watered in well.

Winterizing

In order to prepare your plants for the winter, it is important that no new growth be stimulated for three to five weeks before the first fall frost. You should therefore stop all fertilizing two months before the first frost, and stop dead-heading three to five weeks before the frost date. This procedure allows the plant to harden off naturally and go dormant, and it will reduce damage from winter kill.

Where winter protection is needed, it should be applied after temperatures are regularly below 40° F. Where temperatures do not regularly drop below 20° F during winter, a light protection of leaves or evergreen boughs is sufficient. In colder areas, mound up soil from another part of the garden over the canes to a height of 10–12 inches. Tying the canes together before mounding the soil around them will prevent them from breaking in the wind.

In severely cold winters, some gardeners use a plastic foam rose cone. Place the cone over the plant and weight it with a brick so it will not blow away. Do not cover the cone in any other way, because it needs adequate ventilation to keep insects and diseases from appearing inside. Another way to protect rose bushes in severe cold is to surround the plants with a collar of cardboard, newspaper, or wire mesh and fill the space within the collar with leaves, pine needles, or straw.

Roses grown in containers can be buried in the soil to the top of the container or stored inside a shed or garage where they will not freeze. Keep the soil barely moist during the winter, and cover the plant with a plastic bag to keep it from drying out. Do not move plants inside until they are dormant.

Winter protection should be gradually removed in early spring as signs of growth appear.

Hardiness and the Zone Map

The Plant Hardiness Map on pages 106–107 was prepared by the U.S. Department of Agriculture and divides the country into ten zones, based on minimum winter temperatures. The map can be used as a guideline for the type of winter protection you should apply. As a general rule, it is safe to say that no winter protection will be needed in zones 8, 9, and 10; that moderate methods of winter protection will be needed in zones 5, 6, and 7; and that extreme methods of winter protection will be needed from zone 4 north.

In the individual plant descriptions, a temperature is given to which the plant is normally hardy, and below which protection is needed. During winters where there is no snow cover or where there are high winds, however, roses will be more subject to winter damage.

Bring on the Blossoms

You now have all the information you should need to get started growing beautiful modern roses. Whether you opt for the classic elegance of the hybrid teas, or choose to adorn your patio and terrace with the charm of miniature roses, you will find within these pages just the right flowers for your setting, skill, and temperament. So turn to the individual accounts, and prepare to be the envy of your neighborhood.

Modern Roses

First Edition (Floribunda)

Delbard, 197

This bright floribunda was an All-America Rose Selection in 1977. Long, pointed buds open into a luminous coral flower, shaded in orange. A similar hybrid is Fashion, introduced in 1950 (Boerner), and winner of many awards.

GARDEN PROFILE

First Edition's flowers have a hybrid-tea form. They usually bloom in clusters on short stems, but may be single. First Edition i one of the most reliable repeater among the floribundas, making i excellent as a hedge rose. Doubl flowers with 28 petals are slightl fragrant; they open to 2½–3 inche across. The well-branched, spread ing plants grow 3½–4 feet tall and have moderately thorny canes. Th light green leaves are large and glossy; they have average resistance to disease. Provide winter protec tion below 25° F.

Little Darling (Floribunda)

Duehrsen, 1956

Winner of the Portland Gold Medal in 1958 and the American Rose Society David Fuertenberg Prize in 1964, this slightly fragrant floribunda makes a good hedge or shrub rose. The flowers, a blend of yellow and salmon-pink, are both little and darling, although the plant can be quite large.

GARDEN PROFILE

Blooms are a perfect hybrid-tea form when they first open, finishing in an open, cupped form and appearing in small clusters on arching stems. The flowers are double, 2–2½ inches across, with 24–30 petals, repeating fairly well all summer. The plant grows 3–4 feet tall and is very wide spreading; pruning to an inside bud, which is an exception to the general rule, will keep Little Darling more compact. The leaves are dark green, leathery, and glossy; the canes have small prickles but few thorns. Disease resistance is better than average. Winter protection is needed below 10° F.

Simplicity (Floribunda)

Warriner, 1979

Simplicity is one of the better floribundas for hedging or shrub use, because it grows somewhat taller than many others in its class. It produces showy, medium pink blooms.

GARDEN PROFILE

The double flowers, with 18–2 petals, repeat very quickly all sum mer; blooms are cup shaped to flat opening to 3–4 inches across. The appear in small clusters on long stems. There is a slight fragrance Plants are 4–5 feet tall and quit slender. The canes are moderatel thorny and are covered with me dium green, semiglossy foliage Protection against black spot mus be provided. Protect in winter whe temperatures fall below 15° F.

Angel Face (Floribunda)

Swim & Weeks, 1969

Angel Face was an All-America Selection in 1969 and the recipient of the American Rose Society's John Cook Medal in 1971. A deep mauve floribunda, it also has a climbing form. Like most other roses in its color range, Angel Face is extremely fragrant.

GARDEN PROFILE

The double flowers, which usually bloom in clusters but can appear singly, are 3½–4 inches across and have 35–40 petals. Formal, pointed buds open into informal, flat to slightly cupped blooms that have ruffled petals and showy yellow stamens. Repeat bloom is good throughout the season. Plants grow 2½–3 feet tall and are mounded, spreading, and vigorous. Leaves are dark green, leathery, and semiglossy. The canes are moderately thorny. Angel Face is susceptible to black spot and must have winter protection where temperatures are 20° F or below.

Betty Prior (Floribunda)

Betty Prior is one of the older floribundas, yet it remains one of the best single roses today. Blooms are medium to deep pink and reminiscent of the blossoms of the flowering dogwood.

GARDEN PROFILE

Flowers have 5 petals and open from a cup-shaped bud to a flat bloom 3–3½ inches across. They repe quickly in clusters all summer an are fragrant. Plants are 5–7 feet ta and quite bushy. The medium gree foliage is semiglossy. Canes a moderately thorny. Betty Prior ha average resistance to disease; it winter hardy without protection temperatures of 15° F.

Gene Boerner (Floribunda)

Named for the most famous American hybridizer of floribundas, this rose was an All-America Rose Selection in 1969. Full, hybrid tea-shaped blooms are a clear, medium pink with a slight luminescence.

GARDEN PROFILE

The double flowers have 35 petals and are 3–3½ inches across. They usually appear in large clusters and repeat very quickly throughout the summer. There is a slight, sweet fragrance. Vigorous, slender plants grow 4–5 feet tall and have slightly thorny canes. The foliage, which has average disease resistance, is medium green and semiglossy. Provide winter protection where temperatures drop below 20° F.

Escapade (Floribunda)

Harkness, 196

Because it has 12 petals, Escapade is not a true single rose, but it gives the impression of one, with blooms that open flat to saucer shaped. The pink flowers have a white center.

GARDEN PROFILE

Semidouble blooms are 3–3 inches across and fragrant. They repeat very quickly in clusters a summer. Plants are 2½–3 feet ta and as wide in growth. Canes a slightly thorny and clothed glossy, light to medium green f liage that has better than averag disease resistance. Winter prote tion is necessary below 15° F.

Iceberg (Floribunda)

Kordes, 1958

Known as Schneewittchen in Germany and Fée de Neiges in France, this rose won the Royal National Rose Society Gold Medal in 1958. Its flowers are pure white. Iceberg works extremely well as a hedge rose.

GARDEN PROFILE

Very fragrant, double flowers are 3 inches across and have 30 petals. They are very decorative, opening into cup-shaped blooms that appear in large clusters all summer long. Plants grow 4–5 feet tall and are very wide spreading. Leaves are light green, narrow, and glossy; they need protection from black spot. Protect in winter where temperatures drop below 20° F.

Ivory Fashion (Floribunda)

Boerner, 195

An All-America Rose Selection in 1959, this floribunda has fragrant, creamy white blooms. Its flowers are long lasting on the plant and when cut.

GARDEN PROFILE

Round buds open quickly into fl 3½- to 4-inch, open, semidoub flowers with 15–18 petals. Flowe are fragrant and bloom in cluste reliably throughout the seaso Plants grow 3½–4 feet tall and ha smooth, almost thornless canes. T medium green foliage is leathe and semiglossy, and has average d ease resistance. Ivory Fashion is wi ter hardy to 20° F witho protection.

pricot Nectar (Floribunda)

Boerner, 1966

A n All-America Rose Selection for 1966, Apricot Nectar can disbudded, but when it is left to ow naturally it produces crowded isters of high-centered to cup-aped flowers. Petals are a soft apri-t-pink, with yellow shading at eir bases; the flowers do not fade the sun.

GARDEN PROFILE

Double flowers have 35 petals and are 4–4½ inches across. Blooms are produced heavily all season and have a strong fruity fragrance. The vigorous plants are 3½–4½ feet tall and bushy, making this a good rose for hedging. Canes are smooth with very few thorns. Foliage is medium green and semiglossy; it has average resistance to disease. Apricot Nectar is winter hardy to 20° F, an unusual aspect for a rose in this color class.

Saratoga (Floribunda)

Boerner, 19

An All-America Rose Selection winner for 1964, Saratoga's white blooms resemble those of the gardenia, and are almost as fragrant. Another white floribunda, French Lace (Warriner, 1980), is less fragrant but it produces more even, high-centered blooms.

GARDEN PROFILE

Double flowers with 30–35 pet open to 4 inches across. They hav decorative form and appear in la clusters, repeating fairly w throughout the summer. The we branched, spreading plants grow 3½ feet tall. The canes are mod ately thorny and covered with lig green, leathery, glossy foliage. D ease resistance is average; protect winter below 20° F.

Sun Flare (Floribunda)

An All-America Rose Selection for 1983, Sun Flare is a bright, non-fading yellow rose with an unusual licorice fragrance. Like many floribundas, it looks well in combination with other roses; its bright yellow blooms will add a welcome accent to your garden.

GARDEN PROFILE

The medium yellow, double blooms, with 27–30 petals, open to 2–3 inches across. Repeating singly or in clusters abundantly all season, flowers open with a high center and finish in a cup shape. Spreading plants grow 2–2½ feet tall and have light green, glossy leaves. The plant has better than average disease resistance. Apply winter protection below 15° F.

Impatient (Floribunda)

An All-America Rose Selection for 1984, Impatient has high-centered blooms like a hybrid tea, in bright orange with a yellow base. Another orange floribunda is Orangeade (McGreedy, 1959); it has 7–9 petals and is less winter hardy than Impatient.

GARDEN PROFILE

The slightly fragrant flowers are double, with 20–30 petals, opening to 3 inches across. Blooms appear singly or in small clusters and have fair repeat bloom throughout the season. Plants are well branched and grow 3–3½ feet tall. Canes are very thorny and are covered with dark green, semiglossy leaves. Impatient has average resistance to disease. Protect in winter where temperatures drop below 25° F.

Cathedral (Floribunda)

McGredy, 1975

Known in Europe as Coventry Cathedral, this was an All-America Rose Selection in 1976. The high-centered flowers, which resemble hybrid-tea blooms, are dark apricot to orange, blended with a touch of yellow.

GARDEN PROFILE

Double, waxy flowers have 18–24 petals and open to 4–5 inches across. The slightly fragrant blooms repeat heavily all summer. Bushy plants are 3½–4 feet tall, with moderately thorny canes and olive to dark green, shiny foliage. Disease resistance is average. Provide winter protection below 20° F.

Vogue (Floribunda)

Boerner, 195

An All-America Rose Selection for 1952, Vogue is one of the most famous and popular roses in its class. It also claimed both the Portland Gold Medal and the Geneva Gold Medal in 1950. The flowers are medium to deep coral.

GARDEN PROFILE

Double flowers have 25 petals and a high-centered form like a hybrid tea; they eventually open into blooms 3½–4½ inches wide. Th slightly fragrant flowers general appear in large clusters and repe very well all season. The uprigh well-branched plant grows 4–5 fe tall and has medium green, sem glossy leaves. The canes are mode ately thorny. The plant has avera resistance to disease, but may nee protection against black spot. It winter hardy without protection temperatures of 15° F.

Intrigue (Floribunda)

Warriner, 1984

An All-America Selection for 1984, this compact floribunda has blooms of medium purple that often have a gray cast to the petals. There is another floribunda of the same name with red blooms.

GARDEN PROFILE

Blooms start with a high-centered form, opening into decorative double flowers 3 inches across. Repeat bloom throughout the season is fair to good. The fragrance is strong, a typical feature of roses in this color class. Plants grow 1–2 feet tall, making this a good rose for edges. Canes are moderately thorny and are covered with dark green, shiny foliage. Intrigue has average resistance to disease. Provide winter protection where temperatures fall below 30° F.

Aquarius (Grandiflora)

Armstrong, 1971

Aquarius was an All-America Rose Selection in 1971. Its blooms are large for a grandiflora, especially when it is disbudded. The flowers, a blend of medium and light pink and cream, are very long lasting when cut.

GARDEN PROFILE

Blooms are 3½–4½ inches across, with 35–40 petals. Long, tight buds open into a high-centered, swirled flower; the edges of the petals are darker pink than the bases. Blooming well all summer either in clusters or singly, Aquarius has a slight fragrance. The upright, bushy plant is 4½–5 feet tall and vigorous. Leaves are large, dull medium green, and leathery. Canes are of moderate thorniness. The plant has better than average disease resistance and needs winter protection only below 10° F.

This All-America Rose Selection for 1969 is one of the roses that best fits the definition of a grandiflora—producing abundant blooms with little deviation from the hybrid-tea ideal. Blooms are high centered to cupped, and generally appear in clusters.

GARDEN PROFILE

Double flowers with 35–40 petals are 3–3½ inches across and brick-red to orange-red. Blooming abundantly all season, they have a slight fragrance and are long lasting both on the plant and when cut. The bushy plant grows 4½–5 feet tall and has leathery, medium green leaves with bronze tones. The plant has average disease resistance and is winter hardy to 20° F.

White Lightnin' (Grandiflora)   Swim & Christensen, 198●

Typical of the grandiflora class, this rose has small to medium-sized flowers that generally appear in clusters. White Lightnin' has pure, clear white blooms that are very fragrant.

GARDEN PROFILE

The flowers are double, with 26–32 petals; they measure 3½–4 inches across. White Lightnin' has cupped blooms that repeat well all season. The upright, bushy plant is 4½–5 feet tall and has dark green, glossy foliage with average disease resistance. Canes are moderately thorny. Provide protection in winter where temperatures fall below 25° F.

Pink Parfait (Grandiflora)

Swim, 1960

An All-America Rose Selection for 1961, Pink Parfait also claimed the Portland Gold Medal in 1959 and the Royal National Rose Society Gold Medal in 1962. This rose is a blend of light and medium pink, with the edges of the petals a darker pink than the bases.

GARDEN PROFILE

Flowers are small—just 3 inches across when fully open—and have a slender, high-centered form. Double blooms with 20–25 petals are produced in clusters on long, slender stems throughout the season. They have a slight fragrance. The bushy plant grows 3½–4½ feet tall and has moderately thorny canes. The foliage is medium green, leathery, and semiglossy. Disease resistance is average. Provide winter protection where temperatures fall below 10° F.

Camelot (Grandiflora)

Swim & Weeks, 196

An All-America Rose Selection for 1965, Camelot is particularly pleasing as a long-lasting cut flower. The flowers are coral- to salmon-pink.

GARDEN PROFILE

The cup-shaped flowers are 3½– inches wide with 40–55 petals; th appear in clusters. They repeat we all season and have a spicy fragrance The plant grows 5–5½ feet tall an is quite bushy. The leaves are large dark green, leathery, and glossy; th foliage has better than average di ease resistance. Provide winter pr tection where temperatures dro below 15° F.

Queen Elizabeth (Grandiflora)

Lammerts, 1955

The grandiflora class was created to accommodate this rose. Queen Elizabeth displays a combination of hybrid tea–type flowers and the clustering typical of the floribundas. Queen Elizabeth won many honors; it was an All-America Rose Selection in 1955 and was awarded the Royal National Rose Society Gold Medal the same year, the American Rose Society Gertrude M. Hubbard Gold Medal in 1957, the American Rose Society National Gold Medal Certificate in 1960, and the Golden Rose of The Hague in 1968. It remains very popular.

GARDEN PROFILE

Double, fragrant flowers with 40 petals are either high centered or cupped. They are a light to medium pink, with a slightly darker edge on the petals. Queen Elizabeth blooms abundantly all season on long cutting stems. Typical grandifloras are tall plants, and Queen Elizabeth grows 5–7 feet tall. The canes are almost thornless and foliage is dark green, leathery, and glossy. The plant has better than average disease resistance and is winter hardy without protection to 15° F.

Gold Medal (Grandiflora)

Christensen, 1982

Gold Medal fits the definition of a grandiflora to a T—large flowers on long stems, blooming in clusters. Its blooms are a rich gold, with the edges of the petals tinged in red. The color is at its best in the cool of early summer and fall.

GARDEN PROFILE

The double blooms have 35–40 pe als and hold their classic form we on the plant or when cut. Repeatin well all season long, the flowers ar up to 5 inches across and have slightly fruity or tealike fragranc The plant grows 4½–5½ feet hig and is upright, vigorous, an bushy. The foliage is dark green an semiglossy. Gold Medal is prone t black spot a.id must be protecte from cold where winter tempera tures drop below 30° F.

Prominent (Grandiflora)

Kordes, 1971

With fluorescent orange-red blooms, Prominent stands out. It was an All-America Rose Selection and claimed the Portland Gold Medal in 1977. This rose is known as Korp in Europe.

GARDEN PROFILE

Double blooms are small, 2½–3 inches wide when fully open, and have a classic high-centered or cupped form when first open. Bloom is abundant all summer, and flowers appear singly or in clusters. The flowers, with 30–35 petals, have a slight fragrance. Plants grow 3–4 feet tall and are well branched with thorny canes; they bear dull, dark green, leathery leaves. Disease resistance is average. Plants need winter protection below 20° F.

Pristine (Hybrid Tea)

Warriner, 197

With its white petals edged in delicate pink, Pristine lives up to its name. A similar hybrid is Princesse de Monaco (Meilland, 1981), which has a wider, deeper band of pink edging.

GARDEN PROFILE

The double flowers have 30–35 pe als and are 4½–6 inches acro Pristine blooms well all season, wi flowers one to a stem, and has fa repeat flowering. There is a slig fragrance. The plant, which can la vigor, grows to 4 feet tall and h almost thornless canes. Leaves a very large, dark green, and gloss Pristine has average disease resi tance but needs winter protecti below 25° F.

Garden Party (Hybrid Tea)

Swim, 1959

Garden Party is a classic that was awarded the Bagatelle Gold Medal in 1959 and was an All-America Rose Selection in 1960. It is a pure white, delicately tinted at the petals' edges in pink.

GARDEN PROFILE

Round buds open in large, double blooms 5–5½ inches wide with 25–30 petals in the classic hybrid-tea form. Garden Party is long lasting as a cut flower and has a good fragrance. Plants are well branched and repeat their bloom heavily all season. Large leaves are medium green and glossy. Growing vigorously to 4–5 feet tall, it has better than average resistance to black spot but is prone to mildew. Provide protection in winter below 10° F.

Blue Moon (Hybrid Tea)

Although there may never be a truly blue rose, Blue Moon comes closer than many others. Known as Mainzer Fastnacht in West Germany, where it was hybridized, it is a lavender with definite blue tones. It was awarded the Rome Gold Medal in 1964.

GARDEN PROFILE

The double flowers are 4–4½ inch wide with 40 petals. Blooming reliably all summer, Blue Moon, like most lavender roses, has a strong lemon fragrance. The buds are high centered, opening evenly into rounded bloom. The upright plar grows 4–5 feet tall and is we branched and fairly vigorous. It ha average disease resistance but mus receive winter protection wher temperatures drop below 20° F. Th canes have medium thorniness leaves are medium green and glossy

Kölner Karneval (Hybrid Tea)

Kordes, 1964

This hybrid from West Germany is also sold under the names Cologne Carnival and Blue Girl. Kölner Karneval is one of the most reliably blue-mauve roses available.

Garden Profile

Double flowers with 40 petals are 4½–5½ inches across and repeat well throughout the season. Like all mauve roses, Kölner Karneval is fragrant, although its fragrance is light. It lacks the classic high-centered look, but its cupped form is considered a good hybrid-tea form. It blooms singly or in clusters. The bushy plant grows 2½–3 feet tall and has moderately thorny canes. The leathery foliage is dark green and glossy. It has average disease resistance and is winter hardy to 20° F without protection.

First Prize (Hybrid Tea)

Boerner, 197

A frequent blue-ribbon winner at rose shows, First Prize was an All-America Rose Selection in 1970 and took the American Rose Society Gertrude M. Hubbard Gold Medal in 1971. As a cut flower, it has a long life if cut tight. There is a climbing form.

GARDEN PROFILE

Tall, ivory buds open into ve high-centered flowers that ha ivory at the base of the petal blending into medium pink at th edges. Flowers are double, 5–5 inches wide when fully open, wit 30–35 petals. The fragrant bloom flower well throughout the growin season. Foliage is dark green an leathery. The vigorous, spreadin plant grows 4–5 feet tall but prone to black spot and mildew Provide protection in winter when temperatures fall below 30° F.

Paradise (Hybrid Tea)

Weeks, 1978

Deep mauve with red edges, Paradise represented a breakthrough in color when first hybridized. It was an All-America Rose Selection winner in 1979 and remains unique among rose varieties.

GARDEN PROFILE

Tall buds open into high-centered, slender flowers with a classic hybrid-tea form. The blooms are double, with 25–30 petals, and 3½–4½ inches across when fully open. Paradise repeats well throughout the season and has a pleasant, rich fragrance. Canes are moderately thorny on a 4–4½ foot plant. Foliage is dark green and glossy. Paradise is prone to mildew where climate is cool and damp. Provide winter protection below 20° F.

Tiffany (Hybrid Tea)

Lindquist, 195

After a quarter-century on the market, Tiffany is still one of the more popular hybrid teas. It was an All-America Rose Selection award in 1955 and won the American Rose Society David Fuerstenberg Prize in 1957 and the James Alexander Gamble Rose Fragrance Medal in 1962. The flowers are a medium to deep pink blend, with yellow at the bases of the petals. There is a climbing form of Tiffany.

GARDEN PROFILE

The double flowers are highly fragrant, with 25–30 petals; they open to 4–5 inches wide. As the bud unfurl, the flower has a classic hybrid-tea form. The fragrance is very heavy, and repeat bloom is good Tiffany can bloom singly or in clusters. The very vigorous plant is 4–4½ feet tall and has moderately thorny canes. Foliage is medium to dark green and glossy. Disease resistance is average. Provide winter protection below 25° F.

Charlotte Armstrong (Hybrid Tea)   Lammerts, 1940

Charlotte Armstrong was an All-America Rose Selection in 1941 and received the Portland Gold Medal in 1941, and the Royal National Rose Society Gold Medal in 1950. Named for a family member of one of America's oldest rose nurseries, it remains popular for its brilliant deep pink to light red color. It has been used extensively in hybridizing and is in the parentage of many of today's modern roses. There is also a climbing form of Charlotte Armstrong.

GARDEN PROFILE

The double flowers have a medium fragrance and are 3½–4½ inches wide with 35 petals. Charlotte Armstrong blooms most heavily in early summer, and off and on throughout the season. The red buds are long and slender, opening into loose, informal, slightly flat flowers on long stems. The upright, bushy plant grows 5–6 feet tall and is fairly vigorous. It has average disease resistance and needs winter protection below 20° F. Foliage is large, dark green, and leathery; canes have medium thorniness.

Royal Highness (Hybrid Tea)

Swim & Weeks, 196?

A multiple award winner, Royal Highness was an All-America Rose Selection in 1963 and took the Portland Gold Medal in 1960, the Madrid Gold Medal in 1962, and the American Rose Society David Fuerstenberg Prize in 1964. It is a very pale, delicate pink rose.

GARDEN PROFILE

Slender buds open into narrow high-centered, double flowers wit 40–45 petals. Fully open, it mea sures 5 inches across. Fragrance heavy and repeat bloom is good The upright, bushy plant is 4½– feet tall and has moderately thorn canes. Disease resistance is average but the plant does not tolerate col well; it needs winter protectio below 30° F.

La France (Hybrid Tea)

Guillot Fils, 1867

After more than a century in cultivation, La France is still widely and deservedly popular. Most experts consider it to be the first hybrid tea and the first of the modern roses.

GARDEN PROFILE

Blooms are silvery pink with a brighter pink on the undersides of the petals. Flowers are very double, with 60 petals, and 4–4½ inches across. La France blooms most heavily in early summer and again in fall. It has a high center, although it is slightly more informal-looking than today's hybrid teas. The fragrance is very heavy. Well-branched plants are moderately vigorous and grow 4–5 feet tall. Medium-sized foliage is green and glossy. La France has average disease resistance and is hardy without protection to 20° F in winter.

Pink Favorite (Hybrid Tea)

Van Abrams, 195

Winner of the Portland Gold Medal in 1957, Pink Favorite has a medium pink, decorative flower. Its bright, glossy leaves add a welcome ornamental note to the rose garden.

GARDEN PROFILE
The double blooms with 21–28 pe als are 3½–4 inches wide an bloom heavily all season. They hav a slight fragrance. The form of th flower is loose, cupped, or oper blooms may appear singly but ar usually in clusters. The uprigh plant is 4–4½ feet tall and ha moderately thorny canes. Leaves ar medium green and very glossy. Th plant has average disease resistanc and is hardy without winter protec tion to 20° F.

Peace (Hybrid Tea)

Perhaps the most popular hybrid tea in history, Peace was introduced as the hostilities of World War II drew to a close, and its remarkable beauty created a worldwide sensation. It has received numerous awards; it was an All-America Rose Selection in 1946 and claimed the Portland Gold Medal in 1944, the American Rose Society National Gold Medal Certificate in 1947, The Royal National Rose Society Gold Medal in 1947, and the Golden Rose of The Hague in 1965. The climbing form is one of the tallest and most vigorous climbers.

GARDEN PROFILE

The very large, 6–7-inch blooms are yellow, edged in pink. Flowers are very double, with more than 50 petals, and have a slight fragrance. Peace blooms well in early summer but may be slow to repeat. Flowers are high centered but may have divided centers. The foliage is large, leathery, and very shiny. Canes are moderately thorny. Plants grow 5–6 feet tall and can be prone to black spot. Winter protection is needed below 15° F.

Granada (Hybrid Tea)

Lindquist, 196

Granada is classed by the American Rose Society as a red blend, but is actually a blend of yellow, gold, pink, and red. Winner of the James Alexander Gamble Rose Fragrance Medal in 1968, it has a spicy fragrance and blooms prolifically.

GARDEN PROFILE

The double flowers, with 18–2 petals, are slender, high centered and 3–4 inches wide, opening fror urn-shaped buds. Granada repeat well throughout the season an blooms either singly or in clusters Upright, vigorous, bushy plants ar 4–5 feet tall. Canes are very thorn and covered with dark green, leath ery, crinkled leaves. This rose ha average resistance to black spot bu is prone to mildew. Protect in win ter below 20° F.

Chicago Peace (Hybrid Tea) Johnson, 1962

This sport, or chance mutation, of Peace was discovered by a Chicago gardener; it displays all of that famous rose's good qualities in a deeper color range. Chicago Peace is primarily a deep pink rose with yellow at the base of the petals and blending of yellow, apricot, and lighter tones of pink throughout.

GARDEN PROFILE

The double flowers are 5–5½ inches wide and extremely full, with 50–60 petals. Blooming well all season, Chicago Peace is somewhat flat-topped when open and has a slight fragrance. The upright, vigorous plant grows 4½–5½ feet high and is well branched. It is susceptible to black spot and needs winter protection where temperatures drop below 10° F. Dark green foliage is large, leathery, and glossy, and the canes are moderately thorny.

Duet (Hybrid Tea)

Swim, 196

This dusty coral-pink rose was an All-America Rose Selection in 1961. Generally blooming in clusters, it has a long vase life and therefore is an excellent cut flower.

GARDEN PROFILE

Slim, tall, urn-shaped buds open into 4-inch, double flowers with 25–35 petals. When fully open, Duet is somewhat informal and highly decorative. The mediu coral-pink petals have a slight darker tone on their underside Blooming heavily all season, Du also has a good fragrance. Uprigh slightly spreading plants are vigo ous and 4½–5½ feet tall. Larg leaves are leathery, medium gree and of average disease resistanc Winter-protect where temperatur drop below 20° F.

Michèle Meilland (Hybrid Tea)   Meilland, 1945

Named for one of the members of the Meilland family, famous French hybridizers, Michèle Meilland is a light, delicate pink rose; it is long lasting on the bush or as a cut flower.

GARDEN PROFILE

The flowers are double, with 30–35 petals, and are 3½–4 inches across. Tall buds open into a high-centered flower with classic hybrid-tea form and a slight fragrance. Michèle Meilland blooms well all season. The plants are compact, 3–4 feet high, and have moderately thorny canes. Semiglossy foliage is medium green. It has average disease resistance and is winter hardy to 25° F without protection.

Pink Peace (Hybrid Tea)

Meilland, 19

A descendant of Peace, this rose claimed both the Geneva Gold Medal and the Rome Gold Medal in 1959, the year of its introduction. It is a medium to deep solid pink with a very heavy fragrance.

GARDEN PROFILE

Flowers are very double, with 50–65 petals, and the open bloom can be 6 inches across. Although it can have a high-centered form, Pink Peace more often is rounded to cupped and very decorative. It repeats very well throughout the growing season. The bushy plant grows 4½–5½ feet high and has moderately thorny canes. Leaves are medium green, leathery, and dull. It has better than average disease resistance; winter hardy to 10° F.

Friendship (Hybrid Tea)

Lindquist, 1978

There are more pink roses than roses of any other color, so only the best survive. An All-America Rose Selection for 1979, this clear, deep pink rose has become one of the classics.

GARDEN PROFILE

An excellent cut flower, Friendship has a tall bud that opens into a high-centered, classic hybrid-tea form. It is double, with 25–30 petals, and 4½–5½ inches wide when open. Highly fragrant, it repeats well all season. The upright and vigorous plant is 5–6 feet tall; the large foliage is medium green and shiny. It has average disease resistance. Provide winter protection below 10° F.

Tropicana was the first of the pure orange-red hybrid tea and is still one of the best in its color class. Called Super Star in Europe, it was an All-America Rose Selection in 1963 and won the Bagatelle Gold Medal in 1960, the Royal National Rose Society Gold Medal in 1960, the Geneva Gold Medal and the Portland Gold Medal in 1960, the Golden Rose of The Hague in 1963, and the American Rose Society National Gold Medal Certificate in 1967.

GARDEN PROFILE

Double flowers have 30–35 pet⬤ and a heavy, fruity scent. It has high-centered form, becoming c⬤ shaped and 5 inches across wh⬤ open. The plant is extremely vig⬤ ous and bushy, growing 4–5 f⬤ tall. The foliage is dark gree⬤ leathery, and glossy. Disease res⬤ tance is very good, and the plant winter hardy to 10° F.

Fragrant Cloud (Hybrid Tea)   Tantau, 1963

This orange-red rose has a tinge of dull blue or gray on the petals, and it is very popular for its intense, true rose fragrance (damask). It was acclaimed as winner of the Royal National Rose Society Gold Medal in 1963, the Portland Gold Medal in 1967, and the James Alexander Gamble Rose Fragrance Medal in 1969. In West Germany, where it was hybridized, it is known Duftwolke.

Garden Profile

Flowers of medium orange-red are 3½–4½ inches across and double, with 25–30 petals. High centered as a bud, Fragrant Cloud opens into a flat, full, decorative bloom that repeats well all season, often blooming in clusters. The plant is 3–4 feet tall and compact; foliage is dark green and shiny. It has better than average disease resistance. Provide winter protection below 10° F.

Keepsake (Hybrid Tea)

Kordes, 19

Known in Europe as Esmeralda, Keepsake is a very fragrant variety that blooms well all summer. Like many other hybrid teas, it looks well in a small formal grouping, with walkways dividing the bushes, or with a small statue as a focal point.

Garden Profile

Flowers are light pink on the out sides of the petals, blending int darker pink edges; the insides of th petals are medium to dark pink The double flower has 30–35 petal and opens to 5 inches across Blooming singly or in clusters Keepsake has a cylindrical shape an a high center. The plant is 5–6 fee tall, upright, vigorous, and bushy and has moderately thorny canes The light green foliage is shiny Keepsake has average disease resis tance. Winter protection is neede for temperatures below 10° F.

Electron (Hybrid Tea) McGredy, 1970

Named Mullard Jubilee in Europe, in honor of an electronics company, Electron was an All-America Rose Selection in 1973. It a rich, deep, glowing pink with a very heavy fragrance.

GARDEN PROFILE

Double flowers with 32 petals are 5 inches across, with a perfectly circular form. Electron repeats quickly throughout the season on a vigorous, stocky, slightly spreading 2½- to 3½-foot plant. The canes, covered with medium green, leathery leaves, are extremely thorny; care must be taken when pruning or cutting flowers. It has average disease resistance and is hardy without protection to 20° F.

Chrysler Imperial (Hybrid Tea)

Lammerts, 19

Lauded by many, Chrysler Imperial was an All-America Rose Selection in 1953 and won the Portland Gold Medal in 1951, the American Rose Society John Cook Medal in 1964, and the James Alexander Gamble Rose Fragrance Medal in 1965. This classic has long been popular for its deep red color and typical hybrid-tea form. There is a climbing form.

GARDEN PROFILE

Double flowers have 40–50 peta and repeat very well throughout th growing season. Blooms are 4½– inches wide and have a very heavy true rose (damask) fragrance. Tal pointed buds open into very ful even, high-centered flowers. Vigorous plants are 4–5 feet tall; th moderately thorny canes are heavil clothed with dark green, semigloss leaves. Chrysler Imperial tends t mildew in cool, wet climates bu otherwise has excellent disease resis tance. Provide winter protectio below 10° F.

Christian Dior (Hybrid Tea)

Meilland, 1958

An All-America Rose Selection in 1962, this rose also won the Geneva Gold Medal in 1958, the year of its introduction. It is a clear, medium red, but the edges of the petals can burn and turn dark in hot, dry gardens.

GARDEN PROFILE

Plant Christian Dior where it will receive afternoon shade. The double, medium red flower is 4–4½ inches wide and has fair repeat bloom throughout the season. A formal, high-centered bud opens into a cupped, full flower with 50–60 petals and a slight fragrance. Growing 3½–4½ feet tall, it can be prone to mildew but otherwise has good disease resistance. The canes are almost thornless and have large, medium green, leathery, semiglossy leaves. Protect where temperatures fall below 20° F.

Mon Cheri (Hybrid Tea)

Christensen, 198

An All-America Rose Selection for 1982, Mon Cheri is one of the fastest-repeating roses on the market. It opens from a bright pink bud; the edges of its petals turn deeper red with time and exposure to sunlight.

GARDEN PROFILE

Double blooms are 4½ inches acros and have 30–35 petals. It has a per fect rounded form, but is not hig centered. Fragrance can be light t medium. The compact, slightl spreading plant is 2½–3 feet tall and the canes are moderately thorny the foliage is dark green and glossy Mon Cheri has better than averag disease resistance and is winte hardy without protection to 10° F.

Precious Platinum (Hybrid Tea) Dickson, 1974

This clear, medium red rose makes an excellent cut flower. It is also a good choice if you plant just a few roses, for it is one of the fastest repeating roses you can grow in the garden.

GARDEN PROFILE

Flowers are double, with 35–40 petals, and 3½ inches wide. They have a slight fragrance. The form is typical of the hybrid tea, although the center is not high. Blooms appear singly or in clusters. The vigorous, slightly spreading plant grows 4 feet tall and has moderately thorny canes. Leaves are dark green, leathery, and shiny. Disease resistance is better than average. Provide winter protection below 10° F.

Color Magic (Hybrid Tea)

Warriner, 197

Chosen as an All-America Selection in 1978, this variety has ever-changing colors as individual flowers mature. The buds are ivory, opening into flowers of ivory tinged with pink, which change to dark pink as the flower ages.

GARDEN PROFILE
Large, double, slightly fragrant flowers are 5 inches wide and have 20–30 petals; the bloom repeats well throughout the season. The very even, circular form become cupped as the rose opens, and the color change is intensified by sunlight and high heat. Upright, well branched plants are 3½–4 feet tall and bear large, dark green, semi glossy foliage along moderatel thorny canes. The plant has averag disease resistance, but is not winter hardy without protection when temperatures drop below 30° F.

Mister Lincoln (Hybrid Tea) Swim & Weeks, 1964

An All-America Rose Selection in 1965, Mister Lincoln is still regarded as one of the best red roses. Its petals are a velvety, dark red and do not burn in the sun as easily as other red roses do. There is a climbing form of Mister Lincoln.

GARDEN PROFILE

Very fragrant blooms have 30–40 petals and are 5–5½ inches across. Mister Lincoln repeats well all season and has a high-centered, classic hybrid-tea form on a long cutting stem. The upright plant grows 5–6 feet tall and has dark green, leathery, semiglossy leaves. It has average disease resistance and needs protection below 10° F in winter.

Irish Gold (Hybrid Tea)

Dickson, 196•

Named Grandpa Dickson in Europe, after the patriarch of one of Ireland's oldest rose-breeding families, Irish Gold won the Royal National Rose Society Gold Medal in 1965, the Hague Gold Medal in 1966, and the Golden Rose of The Hague in 1966. Its outer petals quill when the flower is fully open, giving it a star-shaped outline.

GARDEN PROFILE

Double blooms are clear, pale ye low; they sometimes show a pi• edge. Irish Gold has 34 petals; opens to 5–6 inches across and r• peats well all season. The center high and the bloom has a ligh• sweet fragrance. Upright, bush• plants grow 4–4½ feet tall; t• leathery foliage is deep green a• glossy. This rose has average disea• resistance. Winter protection needed below 25° F.

Summer Sunshine (Hybrid Tea) Swim, 1962

Summer Sunshine has more golden-yellow tones than many the other yellow hybrid teas. It is also easier to grow than many others its color range, with more reliable resistance to disease.

GARDEN PROFILE

Blooms are deep yellow, double, with 25–30 petals. Flowers measure 4½–5 inches across and repeat very well all season. Some blooms exhibit a classic hybrid-tea form; others are more cupped and decorative. Fragrance is slight. The plant is vigorous, especially for a yellow rose, and grows 4–5 feet tall. Canes are moderately thorny; foliage is leathery and gray-green. Summer Sunshine is more resistant to disease than many other yellow roses.

King's Ransom (Hybrid Tea)

Morey, 196

An All-America Rose Selection for 1962, King's Ransom is a medium to deep yellow rose with a classic, long bud and flowers whose color does not fade.

GARDEN PROFILE

Double flowers have 35–40 petals and are 4–5 inches wide when open. King's Ransom blooms on long stems and has a pleasant fragranc The flowers, which appear singly in clusters, have a medium-hig center but can be sparse during mi summer. The plant is upright, 4½ 5 feet tall, and has moderate thorny canes. Foliage is light gre and glossy. King's Ransom has go disease resistance but is susceptib to mildew. It needs winter prote tion below 20° F.

utter's Gold (Hybrid Tea) Swim, 1950

utter's Gold was an All-America Rose Selection in 1950, and it ok the Portland Gold Medal in)46, the Bagatelle Gold Medal 1948, the Geneva Gold Medal in)49, and the James Alexander amble Rose Fragrance Medal in)66. It is one of the most highly ented hybrid teas. The flowers are llow, overlaid with orange and ld, and tipped in red.

GARDEN PROFILE

Blooms are tall, slender, and urn shaped. The flowers are double, with 30–35 petals, and 4–5 inches across when fully open. Sutter's Gold repeats quickly all season. The upright plant is 4–4½ feet tall and has moderately thorny canes. Foliage is dark green, leathery, and semiglossy. Disease resistance is average. Provide winter protection below 20° F.

Fred Edmunds (Hybrid Tea)

Meilland, 19

This classic was named for one of America's first professional rose growers and was an All-America Rose Selection in 1944. It also won the Portland Gold Medal in 1942. Flowers are a blend of gold, copper, and orange. There is a climbing form of Fred Edmunds.

GARDEN PROFILE

Double blooms with 20–30 pet open into a cupped or decorati flower 4–5 inches wide. Bloomi well throughout the season, it has very spicy fragrance. When t flower is fully open, it reveals attra tive yellow stamens. The pla grows 3–3½ feet tall in a bush open habit. Canes are moderate thorny and covered with mediu green, leathery, shiny foliage th has average disease resistance. Pr vide winter protection below 20°

Honor (Hybrid Tea)

Warriner, 1980

One of the "wedding trio" (of Love, Honor, and Cherish), this rose was an All-America Rose Selection in 1980. Honor produces white to yellowish-white flowers all season long. It is a good cut flower, with slightly fragrant, long-lasting blooms.

GARDEN PROFILE

Flowers are double, with 20–25 petals, and open to 3–4 inches across. The high-centered to cupped form is loose when fully open. Honor can bloom singly or in clusters. Upright plants grow 4–5 feet tall and have moderately thorny canes. The leathery foliage is large and dark green and of average disease resistance. Honor needs winter protection where temperatures drop below 25° F.

Peaches 'n' Cream (Miniature) Woolcock, 197

Peaches 'n' Cream was awarded the American Rose Society Award of Excellence in 1977. Suitable for bedding and borders, it is also popular for exhibition.

GARDEN PROFILE

Very double flowers have 50 peta and measure 1½ inches across. The are a blend of peachy pink an creamy white and have a slight fra grance; the form is that of the clas sic, high-centered hybrid tea Peaches 'n' Cream has very good re peat bloom throughout the season The bushy plant grows 15–1 inches high and has dark green semiglossy foliage. Disease resis tance is average. Winter protectio is needed below 10° F.

Avandel (Miniature)

Moore, 1977

Avandel won the Award of Excellence from the American Rose Society in 1978. It is as much at home in containers as it is in beds and borders. Its low height also makes it a good edging plant.

GARDEN PROFILE

Long, pointed pink buds open into double yellow flowers blended with peach and pink; they are 1–1½ inches across and have 20–25 pointed petals. The open blooms are flat to cupped. They repeat heavily all summer and have a strong, fruity fragrance. Upright, bushy plants grow 12 inches tall and are relatively disease resistant. Foliage is small, medium to dark green, and leathery. Avandel is winter hardy to temperatures of 0° F.

Popcorn (Miniature)

Morey, 1973

The honey-fragrant Popcorn is one of the most popular white miniatures, with clusters of tiny flowers that actually look like popcorn. This rose is superb for beds, borders, edgings, rock gardens, and container plantings. Another white miniature, Jet Trail (Moore, 1964), has double flowers. It also works beautifully in rock gardens and edgings, as well as in pots indoors over the winter.

GARDEN PROFILE

The single, delicate flowers have 5 petals and are ¾ inch wide. Stamens are yellow and quite showy. Repeat bloom throughout the season is excellent. Popcorn grows 10–14 inches tall and is very compact and rounded. Foliage is medium green, glossy, and of average disease resistance. Protect in winter if temperatures fall below 10° F.

targlo (Miniature)

E. D. Williams, 1973

This white miniature performs beautifully in beds, borders, dgings, and container plantings round patios. It is also a good seection for growing indoors in pots ver winter. Starglo received the American Rose Society Award of xcellence in 1975.

GARDEN PROFILE

The double flowers have 35 petals and are 1¾ inches across; the blooms are white, but they often take on a greenish-yellow tinge. Repeat bloom is good throughout the season. The high-centered blooms have a strong fragrance. Starglo grows to 10–14 inches high and tends to spread along the ground. Leaves are medium green and semiglossy. The plant has average resistance to disease. Protect in winter below 20° F.

Simplex (Miniature)

Moore, 196

A good miniature for beds and borders, Simplex is perhaps the most popular of the single miniature rose varieties. When grown indoors or in cool, cloudy weather, this usually white rose produces pink or yellow blossoms.

GARDEN PROFILE

White flowers have 5 petals openin, flat to reveal showy yellow stamen in the center of the flower. Th bloom is 1¼ inches across and re peats well during the season. Th vigorous plant grows 15–18 inche high and has light green, semigloss foliage. Disease resistance is aver age. Protect in winter where tem peratures fall below 25° F.

Jean Kenneally (Miniature) Bennet, 1984

The pale apricot Jean Kenneally is an excellent miniature for garden beds, borders, edgings, and container plantings. A popular exhibition variety and a good cut rose, it is also good for growing in pots indoors over the winter. It won the American Rose Society Award of Excellence in 1983.

GARDEN PROFILE

The 1½-inch flowers are double, with 24–30 petals. They have a slight fragrance and excellent repeat bloom all season. The apricot-blend flowers open into a classic hybrid-tea form. The bushy plant is 10–16 inches tall and has medium green, semiglossy foliage with average disease resistance. Winter protection is needed below 25° F.

Humdinger (Miniature)

Schwartz, 197⦁

Winner of the American Rose Society Award of Excellence in 1978, Humdinger is so small that it might almost be called a "micro mini." Like Holy Toledo, it is excellent for garden display and also very good in containers.

GARDEN PROFILE

The very double, 1-inch flower⦁ have 50 petals and excellent repea⦁ bloom. The orange-red blooms hav⦁ a classic hybrid-tea form, with pet⦁ als unfurling evenly from a high center. The plant grows only 8–1⦁ inches tall and is quite bushy an⦁ compact. Leaves are dark green an⦁ glossy, and have average disease re⦁ sistance. Protect in winter wher⦁ temperatures fall below 20° F.

tarina (Miniature)   Meilland, 1965

tarina's unusually bright orange-red blooms have made it per- ps the most popular exhibition niature rose of all. The most dely sold of any miniature vari- , Starina is the standard-bearer in color class of miniatures. For ny years, the American Rose So- ty has given Starina the highest ing of all roses. It is a good cut ver.

GARDEN PROFILE

The orange-red flowers, with a touch of yellow at the base of the petals, are double and 1½ inches across. The 35 petals unfurl into a perfect, high-centered form. Starina blooms in midseason with excellent repeat. The bushy, compact plants are 12–16 inches high and have dark green, semiglossy foliage. Disease resistance is better than average. Protect in winter at temperatures below 15° F.

Zinger looks like a tiny single rose, with its flat, red petals setting off the yellow stamens. Despite this effect in the garden landscape, Zinger is actually a semidouble rose. This miniature makes a pleasant garden addition, suitable for edging, borders, and bedding.

GARDEN PROFILE

Flowers semidouble, with 12– petals, measuring 1½ inches acro They are medium red and may h a slight fragrance. Blooms open to reveal showy yellow stamens the center of the flower. Zin, blooms at midseason with good peat. Leaves are medium to d. green and glossy. Zinger has aver resistance to disease. Protect in w ter below 20° F.

ricket (Miniature)

Excellent for planting in garden beds and borders, Cricket is good for container planting and patio display. Another orange miniature is Chattem Centennial (Betty Ady, 1979), a prolific bloomer indoors or out, with a slightly fruity fragrance.

GARDEN PROFILE

The 1¼-inch, double flowers have 25 petals and repeat well over the season. The high-centered to cupped blooms, orange blended with yellow, have a slight fragrance. The plants are bushy, to 14 inches tall; they have dark green, semi-glossy foliage. Cricket has average resistance to disease and should receive winter protection where temperatures drop below 20° F.

Mary Marshall (Miniature)

Named for an avid amateur rose grower, Mary Marshall won the American Rose Society Award of Excellence in 1975. It is excellent for garden display and popular in exhibitions and as a cut flower. There is also a climbing form.

GARDEN PROFILE

The flowers, 1½ inches wide, deep coral with pink, yellow, orange overtones; the blooms double, with 24–30 petals, have the classic hybrid-tea for Fragrance is slight and repeat blo is good. The bushy plant grows 1 14 inches tall; the climbing fo can reach 5 feet. Medium gree semiglossy leaves cover the pl and have better than average dise resistance. Protect in winter wh temperatures fall below 10° F.

Holy Toledo (Miniature)

Christensen, 1979

Winner of the American Rose Society Award of Excellence in 1980, Holy Toledo is suitable for beds and borders and is also a popular exhibition miniature. Hula Girl (E. D. Williams, 1975) and Hot Shot (Bennet, 1982) are also good miniatures in the orange to apricot color range. Both have won the American Rose Society Award of Excellence.

GARDEN PROFILE

Double flowers with 25 petals are 1¾ inches across and are a bright orange to deep apricot, with a yellow base. They repeat very well throughout the season and have a slight fragrance. Buds open into a classic hybrid tea–type form, unfurling evenly from a high center. The vigorous, bushy plant is 18–24 inches tall and has dark green, glossy foliage with better than average disease resistance. Protect in winter where temperatures fall below 30° F.

Rosa roulettii (Miniature)

Many rosarians believe that all modern miniatures are descended from this rose. Also known as *Rosa chinensis minima,* this pink miniature is thought by some to be the same as Pompon de Paris (1839), but the latter is held to be a more double rose. Some experts favor classifying this with the Chinas (in the old garden roses) rather than with the miniatures.

GARDEN PROFILE

Double, deep pink flowers have 20–30 petals and are ¾–1 inch wide. The blooms are decorative and cup-shaped, with slight fragrance and good repeat bloom. The bushy plant grows 15–18 inches high and has medium green, glossy foliage. Some protection may be needed against disease. Provide winter protection below 30° F.

This little rose was among the original striped miniature oses, and still perhaps is the most opular. It performs well in the garen or in a hanging basket, and is a opular show rose. There is delightul variety in its blooms: no two will ver be exactly the same.

GARDEN PROFILE

Semidouble flowers with 14 petals are 1¾ inches wide and have red-and-white stripes. The flowers are cup shaped to open, appearing at midseason with good repeat bloom. Fragrance is slight. The plant grows 10–14 inches high and spreads to 36 inches across. Foliage is medium green to dark green, and semiglossy. Stars 'n' Stripes has average resistance to disease. Protect in winter below 20° F.

Magic Carrousel (Miniature)

Moore, 197

Winner of the American Rose Society Award of Excellence in 1975, Magic Carrousel is well suited to use in beds and borders, where its bright red-and-white blooms will stand out. It also is a popular show variety.

GARDEN PROFILE

Flowers, 1¾–2 inches across, a semidouble with 12–20 petal Blooms are white with red edges the petals and have a very slight fr grance. The flower opens flat cupped, with rounded petals, ar repeats very well through the se son. Magic Carrousel can be amon the tallest of the miniatures, ofte reaching 30 inches. It is very vigo ous, with medium green to bronz glossy leaves. It is more disease r sistant than many others. Wint protection is needed below 10° F.

Rosmarin (Miniature)

Kordes, 1965

Rosmarin is an outstanding variety for beds, borders, and edgings. It blooms abundantly on a compact, rounded plant. Rosmarin more winter hardy than most ther miniatures.

GARDEN PROFILE

Flowers are a pink-and-white blend with excellent repeat bloom. The double blooms, 1½ inches wide, have 35 petals. Fragrant buds open into a decorative, cup-shaped flower. The plants are very vigorous, growing 15–18 inches tall. They bear medium green, semiglossy foliage. Rosmarin has average resistance to disease. Winter protection is needed below 5° F.

Toy Clown (Miniature)

Moore, 196

This popular exhibition variety claimed the American Rose Society Award of Excellence in 1975. Toy Clown grows well both outdoors and indoors, in containers, in beds, and in borders.

GARDEN PROFILE

Semidouble flowers, with 12–2 white, red-edged petals, are 1¹ inches wide. The pointed buds a first cupped and then open fla there may be a slight fragrance. To Clown blooms in midseason wit good repeat. The leaves are a dul dark green edged in red. The plan grows to 10–14 inches and tends t spread. Disease resistance is averag Protect in winter below 20° F.

Dreamglo (Miniature)

An excellent plant for bedding and borders, Dreamglo is also popular exhibition miniature. A similar miniature with pink and white blossoms is Charmglo (E. D. Williams, 1980); it does well in rock gardens and edgings, as well as in borders or containers.

GARDEN PROFILE

Dreamglo bears 1-inch white flowers with red edges on long stems; the blooms have a slight fragrance. They are very double, with 50 petals opening from pointed buds into a very full, classic hybrid-tea form, with petals unfurling from a high center. Repeat bloom is good throughout the season, and the color does not fade in the heat. The tall, vigorous plant is 18–24 inches high and has medium green to dark green, semiglossy foliage. Disease resistance is average. Winter protection is needed below 20° F.

Beauty Secret (Miniature)

A classic hybrid tea in miniature. Winner of the American Rose Society Award of Excellence in 1975, this very fragrant miniature rose is good for garden beds and borders, edgings, and containers. It also grows well indoors in pots over the winter.

GARDEN PROFILE

The flowers are 1½ inches wide medium red, and double, with 24 30 petals. Beauty Secret has excel lent repeat bloom throughout th season. The upright, vigorous bushy plant grows 10–18 inches tal and is clothed in medium to dar green, semiglossy foliage. It has av erage resistance to disease and need winter protection when tempera tures fall below 20° F.

Chipper (Miniature)

A miniature rose that has remained popular despite the creation of thousands of new varieties, Chipper is excellent for garden display and also good in a pot indoors over the winter.

GARDEN PROFILE

Salmon-pink to coral blooms are 1¼ inch wide and have excellent repeat bloom all season long. The double flowers, which have a cupped form, have 24–30 petals and a slight fragrance. Vigorous plants grow 10–14 inches tall and have dark green, leathery, shiny foliage. Chipper has average resistance to disease. Protect in winter below 20° F.

Rainbow's End (Miniature)

Saville, 198

A perfect choice for beds, borders, and edgings, and suitable for container plantings, this yellow-blend miniature rose is good for growing in pots indoors over winter as well. Rainbow's End won the American Rose Society Award of Excellence in 1986.

GARDEN PROFILE

The double flowers have 24–30 petals and are 1½ inches wide. Blooms are yellow, shading to deep pink and red at the edges of the petals. The blooms of plants grown indoors are pure yellow. Buds open into classic hybrid tea–type flowers with good repeat bloom and very slight fragrance. Dark green, glossy foliage covers the bushy plant, which grows to 10–14 inches and has average resistance to disease. Protect in winter below 20° F.

APPENDICES

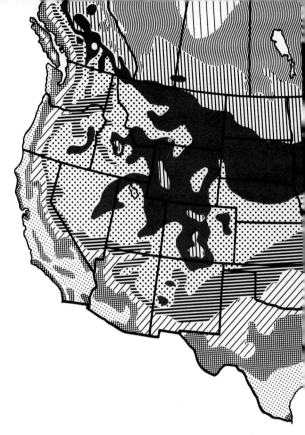

Map: Paul Singer

HARDINESS ZONE MAP

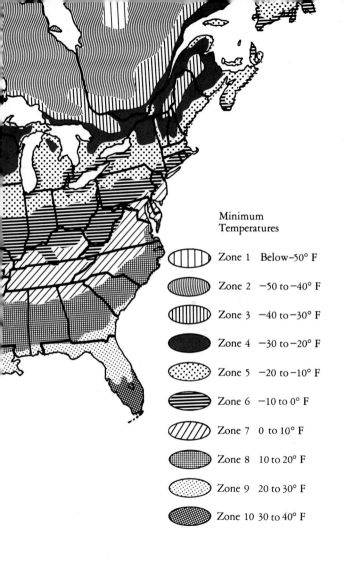

Minimum
Temperatures

Zone 1   Below −50° F

Zone 2   −50 to −40° F

Zone 3   −40 to −30° F

Zone 4   −30 to −20° F

Zone 5   −20 to −10° F

Zone 6   −10 to 0° F

Zone 7   0 to 10° F

Zone 8   10 to 20° F

Zone 9   20 to 30° F

Zone 10 30 to 40° F

GARDEN PESTS AND DISEASES

PLANT DISEASES, insects, and other pests are a fact of life for a gardener. No matter what you grow or how large your garden, it is helpful to become familiar with the common problems in your area and to learn how to control them. Since the general symptoms of plant problems—yellowing of leaves, death or disappearance of plant parts, stunting, poor growth, and wilting—can be caused by a multitude of diseases or pests, some experience is needed to determine which culprit is attacking your roses.

Diseases

Fungi and bacteria cause a variety of diseases, ranging from leaf spots and wilts to root rot, but bacterial diseases usually make the affected plant tissues appear wetter than fungi do. Viruses and mycoplasma are microorganisms too small to be seen with an ordinary microscope. They are often transmitted by insects, such as aphids and leafhoppers, and cause mottled yellow or deformed leaves and stunted growth. Nematodes are microscopic roundworms that usually live in association with plant roots; they cause stunting and poor growth, and sometimes produce galls on leaves. The way a particular disease organism has spread to your roses influences the control measures you may need to take.

Insects and Other Pests

Roses attract many different kinds of insects. Sap-sucking insects—including aphids, leafhoppers, and scale insects—suck plant juices, leaving the victim yellow, stunted, and misshapen. They also produce honeydew, a sticky substance that attracts ants and sooty mold fungus. Thrips and spider mites scrape plant tissue and suck the juices that well up in the injured areas. Beetles and caterpillars consume leaves, whole or in part. Borers tunnel into shoots and stems, where they deposit their eggs; the larvae that hatch feed on plant tissue. Some insects, such as grubs and maggots, are rarely seen above ground. They are destructive nonetheless, because they feed on roots, weakening or killing the plant.

Environmental Stresses

Some plant injuries are caused by severe weather conditions, salt toxicity, rodents, nutritional deficiencies or excesses, pesticides, or damage from lawn mowers. You can avoid many of these injuries by being aware of potential dangers and taking proper precautions.

Methods of Control

Controlling plant pests and diseases is not as overwhelming a task as it may seem. Many of the measures, performed on a day-to-day basis, are preventive, so that you don't have to rely on pesticides that may not be very effective once a culprit has attacked your roses. Observe plants each week for signs of trouble. That way you can prevent or limit a disease or infestation in the early stages.

Your normal gardening routine should include preventive measures. By cultivating the soil regularly, you expose insect and disease-causing organisms to the sun and thus lessen their chances of survival. In the fall, destroy infested and diseased canes, remove dead leaves and flowers, and clean up plant debris. Do not add diseased or infested material to the compost pile. Spray plants with water to dislodge insects and remove suffocating dust. Pick off larger insects by hand. To discourage fungal leaf spots and blights, water plants in the morning and allow leaves to dry off before nightfall. For the same reason, provide adequate air circulation around leaves and stems by giving plants sufficient space.

Always buy healthy, certified, disease-free plants. Check leaves and canes for dead areas and for off-color and stunted tissue. Make sure that your roses are properly cared for.

Insecticides and Fungicides

Weeds provide a home for insects and diseases, so pull them up or use herbicides. Be careful near roses, however, since they are very sensitive to weed-killers. Herbicide injury may cause elongated, straplike, or downward-cupping leaves. Do not apply herbicides, including "weed-and-feed" lawn preparations, too close to flower beds. Spray weed-killers only when there is little air movement, but not on a very hot, dry day.

To protect plant tissue from damage done by insects and diseases, you may choose from among the many insecticides and fungicides that are available. Few products, however, can control diseases that result from bacteria, viruses, and mycoplasma.

Pesticides are usually either "protectant" or "systemic" in nature. Protectants ward off insects or disease organisms from uninfected foliage, while systemics can move through the plant and provide therapeutic or eradicant action as well as protection. Botanical insecticides such as pyrethrum and rotenone have a shorter residual effect on pests, but are considered generally safer for the user and the environment than inorganic chemical insecticides.

Biological control through the use of organisms like *Bacillus thuringiensis* (a bacterium toxic to moth and butterfly larvae) is effective and safe. Recommended pesticides may vary to some extent from region to region, so consult your local Agricultural Experiment Station or plant professional about the appropriate material to use. Always read the pesticide label to be sure that it is registered for use on roses and on the pest with which you are dealing. Follow the label recommendations regarding safety precautions, dosage, and frequency of application. Learn about the life cycle of the pest, so that you know when to begin—and when to stop—spraying.

ARRANGING CUT ROSES

ARRANGERS CALL the rose the "complete flower" because it provides all stages of bloom for a complete arrangement. The rose is adaptable to every occasion: It can be formal when used for weddings, in churches, and at formal teas and showers; and it can be informal any place at home, on the porch or patio, and on the office desk. Moreover, roses are suitable for all types and styles of containers; the old rule that roses should be arranged only in silver or crystal was discarded long ago. People now realize that roses are for everyone and for any setting, and they are today the most popular flower worldwide.

Gathering Roses

Before cutting roses, select the container that will hold them, and try to decide where you will be placing it. If you are a beginner, select a low bowl or horizontal container; one that is about 10 inches in diameter and 2 inches deep will do nicely. You will want to cut your roses early in the morning or after sundown in the evening. They will keep longer if the plants are thoroughly watered one-half day before cutting; make sure to water the soil deeply around the bushes.

Take a pail of cold water with you into the garden. Using sharp rose pruners, cut the stems on a slant, selecting the proper stem length for the container you will be using. Choose strong stems, some with tight buds, some one-quarter open, and the remaining ones one-half and two-thirds open. Clean the foliage with a damp paper napkin or soft cloth (not nylon), and then dry it. Place the roses in a cool place, preferably in a refrigerator at 38° to 40° F—they will keep for days in there. If you have an old refrigerator, you are in luck—the new, self-defrosting models will remove moisture from flowers and thus cause early aging.

In these early stages of rose preparation, remove most thorns and some foliage, especially thorns and foliage below the water line. Rose foliage may be added later if the arrangement calls for it.

Beginning the Arrangement

To establish the proper proportion from the start, choose a stem that is 50 percent longer than your bowl; if your bowl is 8 inches long, your stem should be 12 inches. Using a sharp needlepoint secured with floral clay, place the first stem upright, toward the left side of the bowl. Choose a second stem, approximately three-fourths the length of the first, with the bloom one-fourth to one-third open. Put it firmly in the needlepoint, slanted to the left at an angle of about 45 degrees. The third stem should be about three-fourths the length of the second stem, with the bloom two-thirds or three-fourths open. The third stem should be at a 60-degree angle to the right and in front, with the bloom lower than the bloom on the second stem. This solid, three-stem, three-position, triangular design serves as a basic foundation for a completed arrangement. You may use other lengths of roses or other foliage or flowers to fill in and complete the plan.

Make certain that all your containers, water, and plant material are clean. You may use oasis for arrangements (well soaked before using) if you do not expect the arrangement to last more than one day. If you want to use oasis for a longer period, you must recut the stems (on a slant) and add more cold water. Be sure to use good sharp needlepoints large enough to provide adequate space for the foliage stems and flowers. If some stems are too short, try using florists' picks (small vials filled with water).

A word of caution: Never place cut roses in hot water, since they will not last. Clean cold water in clean containers is all you need to preserve the roses and all plant materials. (Flower preservatives seem to help the arranger more than the flowers themselves.) Change the water and cut the stems a little each day, otherwise, the stems may become clogged and decay. Keep cut roses out of the sun. With this care, cut roses will last a week or longer.

Design Tips

Distinction is the quality all good designers strive for. It may be the result of imagination, originality, beauty, or the use of usual materials in an unusual manner. But one factor common to all distinctive designs is good grooming—that is, attention to detail in handling and preparing roses.

Learn to master mechanical techniques, keeping in mind that, in the final analysis, simplicity is a key concept. "When in doubt, leave it out" is an old but excellent rule for new and advanced arrangers alike. Don't use too much plant material; don't feel that you must put in all the flowers and foliage that you have on hand. Many times it is wise to make the arrangement, leave it for a while, then return to look at it. You will often then see some changes to be made, and most of the time you'll remove or change some of the flowers. Looking at the design through the lens of a camera is often a good way to get a fresh idea of what your arrangement needs. Other factors to consider in your choice of arrangement style or design are the kinds and sizes of other plant materials and your containers. You will also want to think about color values (lightness or darkness) and other qualities such as shapes, silhouettes, contours, and textures.

Consider also the space the arrangement will occupy. For example, if the arrangement is for a mantel, complete the design at that height in order to visualize everything from that vantage point. If it will be placed on a table, work on the design at a table or at the same height. If it is an arrangement for a church or auditorium, sit down at the far end of a room to look at your finished design. By seeing the design from the vantage point from which others will ultimately see it, you will often find ways to improve the design or placement of your arrangement.

Color

Be sure the colors of your flowers do not clash, but blend and complement each other. Remember that some colors—such as mauve, blue, and purple—recede. Use bold, bright tones in a large area. White is lovely in a church and in some auditoriums, but it needs a suitable background to be fully enjoyed. A polychromatic scheme is often appropriate for mass arrangements, whereas a monochromatic one, or a design with variations of one hue, is suitable when particular subtlety or elegance is needed.

The Influence of Geometry

Certain visual elements create certain moods. Horizontal lines suggest peace and tranquillity; vertical lines produce a sense of energy; and diagonal lines are dynamic, restless, and force-ful—use these lines with restraint. A circle or oval conveys a restful or passive mood; triangles create a sense of stability. Curved lines are gracious and flexible, but avoid drooping curves, which imply instability and weakness. Bear in mind, of course, that these geometric patterns are merely a way of classifying designs. A good design does not necessarily follow a geometric pattern.

Matching Design and Placement

If the arrangement is to be placed on a dining table, be sure to finish the arrangement on both sides, front and back. Never make a table arrangement that will block a person's view. If the arrangement is for a buffet table, it may be seen from only one side, so it is not necessary to finish the back; however, you may want to use large leaves or foliage to add depth to the arrangement, as depth is important to the completeness of any design.

Healthy Roses Make Good Arrangements

Remember that good culture pays off. No matter how exquisite your arrangement, if your roses have been neglected or improperly cared for, they will not do justice to your design. It is vital to put the same effort into cultivation—proper planting, pruning, watering, and fertilizing—that you do into arranging your roses once they are cut.

Buying Containers and Vases

If you are going to purchase containers for arrangements, consider the colors and types of roses and other plant material that you will often be using. Soft, subdued pottery in a neutral color is always a fine choice. For arrangements that will look well in a gray container, use something made of lead, pewter, or silver. For yellow flowers, try gold, bronze, or brass. To bring out the orange, go with copper. Baskets are good, too, and interestingly shaped bottles lend themselves to exciting arrangements. Wooden and woven trays also suit many types of arrangements. Vases and containers with unexpected potential may be found at flea markets, Goodwill shops, thrift shops, and garage sales. Once you start arranging, you will find unusual containers for all types of designs.

Flowers and Foliages for Arrangements

Many flowers and foliages go very well with roses. Try the following: daisies, gerberas, snapdragons, love-in-a-mist (*Ni-*

gella), larkspur, delphinium (all colors), lilies (be sure they are in proportion with the size of roses you are using), gladiolus, lupine, tritoma, and veronica. Dried allium blossoms sprayed with gold or silver are like tiny stars on the stem and make beautiful arrangements with roses at Christmastime; place some holly at the base of the arrangement for a lovely holiday touch. You will find many other interesting flowers for arranging with roses.

Line Materials in Arrangements

In arranging roses, it is important to use materials that serve to extend or enhance the line within the arrangement. Line materials include: equistum (a horse tail rush); mullein (flower or seed stem); corn stalks (green or brown); forsythia (green or brown); okra stalks (green or mature); sea oats; pampas grass plumes; wild grasses; Scotch broom; wheat; *spuria* iris foliage; dried burdock; cattails; sanseveria; yucca; and Queen Anne's lace (wild carrot). Vines can often be used when a free-flowing or loose line is needed. Some vines that can be used are: ivy (English, glacier, curly, porcelain, and grape); honeysuckle; grapevine (remove the foliage); wisteria (dried and peeled, with leaves recently removed; it will add a lovely white to an arrangement); white hemlock or circuta (dried); bittersweet; and clematis (with seed pods).

Some large leaves, including the following, are used quite frequently in mass or line arrangements: hosta, canna, calla lily, saxifrage, hydrangea (dried), and fantail willow *(Salix).* Hydrangea blossoms may also be used; try blue hydrangea blooms with blue-red roses. Some arrangements call for branches from trees and shrubs, such as Japanese quince; holly (Chinese or American); red plum; Japanese maple; Japanese fantail willow; tamarix (gives roses an airy feeling); pussy willow; white pine; cork bark *(Euonymus alatus);* highbush cranberry *(Viburnum americana);* and nandina. Trim excess leaves from branches. With some branches, such as cork bark or fantail willow, you can remove all foliage from the branches in order to reveal interesting lines, forms, colors, and textures.

Other Ideas for Arrangements

You can create distinctive rose arrangements by using feathers (especially pheasant or grouse), interesting stones or rocks, dried fungi, and unusual pieces of weathered wood or driftwood. Once you start arranging, you will find beauty in the out-of-doors that you have never really seen or noticed before.

GLOSSARY

Anchor root
A large root serving mainly to hold a plant in place in the soil.

Anther
The terminal part of a stamen, containing the pollen sacs.

Basal cane
One of the main canes of a rose bush, originating from the bud union.

Bud eye
A dormant bud in the axil of a leaf, used for propagation in bud-grafting. Also called an eye.

Bud union
The junction, usually swollen, between the understock and the top variety grafted to it, at or near soil level.

Budded
Propagated from a bud eye.

Button center
A round center in a rose blossom, formed by unexpanded petaloids in the very double roses.

Calyx
Collectively, the sepals of a flower.

Calyx tube
A tube formed partly by the united bases of the sepals and partly by the receptacle.

Confused center
A flower center whose petals are disorganized, not forming a pattern.

Corolla
Collectively, the petals of a flower.

Crown
The region of the bud union, the point near soil level where the top variety and the understock are joined.

Cultivar
A man-made variety of a plant, maintained by vegetative propagation rather than from seed.

Cupped form
In a rose bloom, having an open center, with the stamens visible.

Dead-heading
Removal of old flowers during the growing season to encourage the development of new flowers.

Disbudded
Having the side buds removed to encourage the growth of the flower at the tip of the stem.

Double
Having 24 to 50 petals.

Eye
See Bud eye.

Feeder root
One of the numerous small roots of a plant, through which moisture and nutrients are absorbed from the soil.

Filament
The threadlike lower portion of a stamen, bearing the anther.

Floriferous
Blooming profusely.

Guard petals
The outer petals of a rose, especially when these are larger than the inner petals and enclose them.

High-centered
Having the central petals longest; the classic hybrid tea·rose form.

Hip
The closed and ripened receptacle of a rose, containing the seeds, and often brightly colored.

Lateral cane
A branch of a basal cane.

Leaf axil
The angle between a petiole and the stem to which it is attached.

Leaflet
One of the leaflike parts of a compound leaf.

Main shoot
A basal cane or a strong lateral cane.

Muddled center
A flower center whose petals are disorganized, not forming a pattern. A term applied to old garden roses.

Ovary
The swollen base of a pistil, in which one or more seeds develop.

Petal
One of a series of flower parts lying within the sepals and outside the stamens and pistils; in roses, the petals are large and brightly colored. Collectively termed the corolla.

Petaloids
Small, very short petals located near the center of a flower.

Petiole
The stalk of a leaf.

Pistil
The female reproductive organ of a flower, consisting of an ovary, a style, and a stigma.

Quartered
Having petals arranged in three, four, or five radial segments.

Retentive sepals
Sepals that remain attached to the apex of the receptacle after it has ripened into a hip.

Rhachis
The central axis of a compound leaf, to which the leaflets are attached.

Rootstock
See Understock.

Rugose
Having the leaf veins deeply etched into the upper surface of the leaf.

Semidouble
Having 12 to 24 petals.

Single
Of flowers, having 5 to 12 petals. Of varieties, having only one bloom per stem.

Sport
An abrupt, naturally occurring genetic change resulting in a branch that differs in appearance from the rest of the plant, or, a plant derived by propagation from such a genetically changed branch. Also called a mutation.

Stamen
The male reproductive organ of a flower, consisting of a filament and a pollen-bearing anther.

Stem
A branch of a cane, emerging from a bud eye and bearing leaves and at least one flower.

Stigma
The terminal portion of a pistil, consisting of a sticky surface to which pollen grains adhere during pollination.

Stipule
A small, leaflike appendage at the base of the petiole of a leaf.

Style
The columnar portion of a pistil, extending between the ovary and the stigma.

Sucker
A young cane emerging below the bud union and therefore representing the variety of the understock rather than the top variety.

Top variety
The variety bud-grafted to the understock, and thus the variety that will be represented by the flowers.

Understock
The plant providing the root system to which the top variety is attached in bud-grafting. Also called a rootstock.

Very double
Having more than 50 petals.

PHOTO CREDITS

Armstrong Roses, 93, 95

Gillian Beckett, 35, 70

Sonja Bullaty and Angelo Lomeo ©, 66

The Conard-Pyle Co., 103

Derek Fell, 62, 80

P. A. Haring, 27, 33, 48, 49, 51, 52, 53, 55, 72, 75, 79, 81, 85, 87, 89, 90, 91, 92, 97, 101, 102

Pamela J. Harper, 29, 30, 31, 36, 41, 43, 44, 46, 47, 54, 57, 59, 65, 67, 69, 73, 76, 78, 84, 86, 98, 100

Walter H. Hodge, 38, 39, 50, 58, 82

Ann Reilly, 32, 94

Ann Reilly, PHOTO/NATS, Cover, 2, 25

Joy Spurr, 26, 28, 34, 37, 40, 45, 60, 64, 71, 74, 77, 83, 88, 96, 99, 104

Doug Wechsler, 42, 56, 61, 63, 68

INDEX

CHANTICLEER PRESS
STEWART, TABORI & CHANG

Publisher
ANDREW STEWART

Senior Editor
ANN WHITMAN

Production
KATHY ROSENBLOOM
KARYN SLUTSKY

Design
JOSEPH RUTT